DRITA

An Albanian Girl Discovers Her Ancestors' Faith

By Renée Ritsi

Illustrated by Cameron Thorp

Conciliar Press Ministries, Ben Lomond, California

Drita: An Albanian Girl Discovers Her Ancestors' Faith

Published by Conciliar Press Ministries, Inc.
P.O. Box 76, Ben Lomond, California

Printed in China

ISBN: 978-1-888212-94-5

DEDICATION

This book is dedicated to all the women whose faith has been a light to me and to those around them, especially Sister Galini, Sister Fevronia, Sister Argyro, my grandmother Marianthy, my mother Evangeline, and Lynette Hoppe, who dedicated her life to mission work in Albania.

It was early in the morning. Drita was snuggled under a warm blanket on the living room couch. Outside, she heard the sounds and smells of the city. People talked and laughed. Bells on bicycles rang. Buses chugged and honked. The delicious smell of roasting coffee drifted through her open window. In the distance, horses' hooves clopped as the trash collectors tossed trash onto their wagons.

Inside their apartment Drita heard the familiar sounds of her parents and older brother, Artan, in the kitchen. These were the sounds and smells that she loved.

For a moment Drita thought about the changes that had happened to her beloved country. During the time when the old government was in power, Drita remembered that everyone rode the bus or the train or walked. Then came the revolution. Angry people knocked down statues and demanded a new government. For almost a whole year, no one went to school or work.

Now there was a new government. People had their own cars, and shops and stores were open again. School was also back in session and everyone had brand-new books and pencils.

Suddenly Drita jumped up because she remembered that today was a special day. Inside she felt excited and happy. For months she had gone to catechism class, where a missionary had taught her many beautiful things. She

knew about the birth of Jesus in a simple cave, and His glorious Resurrection from the tomb. She had studied the sacraments and the beautiful history of the Orthodox Church. She could say the prayer *"Ati ynë"* (Our Father) and the *"Besorja"* (I believe). Every night she read her mother's Bible and said her evening prayers. Yes, today was a special day because Drita was going to be baptized.

Drita washed her face, brushed her teeth, and put on her nicest dress.

"*Mami*," she said, "I am ready. Today I will be a Christian like you and *Babi* and *Gjyshi* and *Nëna*. We can take Holy Communion together. *Hajde, Babi,* let's go."

Every summer Drita and her brother Artan stayed with their grandparents, Gjyshi (pronounced ju-shi) and Nëna, in the mountain village where they lived. As Drita walked to church, her mind drifted back to last summer. That was when she first heard about the Orthodox Church.

L ast summer began just like every other. First there was the long bus ride—bumping and stopping and bumping and starting. Then there was the steep walk up the mountain road to their grandparents' village.

The fresh clean air in the village always smelled so sweet, and the water tasted better there than any place in the world. All summer Drita and Artan helped with the chores and took care of *Shega* the donkey. Each morning Drita and Nëna woke up before the men and carried their water containers to the village well. Along the way, Nëna told Drita wonderful stories that she had never heard in school. Her favorite was about a man named Paul.

Paul liked to travel and teach his new friends to love each other. One time Paul was shipwrecked. Another time he was sent to prison. Nëna made it sound so exciting that Drita wanted to go on long, dangerous journeys just like Paul.

Drita loved to hear her grandmother tell story after story as they filled up the containers and carried them back home so they could cook and clean.

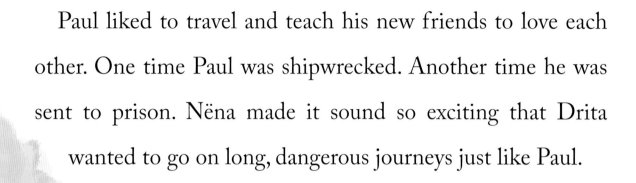

Almost every morning Gjyshi worked at the cooperative. He helped grind wheat into flour, which was sent to the city to make bread. In the afternoon, tired and covered with flour, Drita loved to hold Gjyshi's shirt and shake it so that a cloud of white would surround the two of them.

During the day Drita stayed with her grandmother as she made yogurt and *gjizë* from goat's milk. She would polish the leather straps that held the wooden saddle on Shega the donkey. Best of all she loved to go with her grandparents into the village on Gjyshi's day off.

First, Gjyshi would brush Shega. Then he loaded the baskets that Shega carried. Finally, Gjyshi took Shega's rope and the journey began. Beautiful pine trees and small wildflowers lined the path. Along the way, Gjyshi told stories about proud Albanian heroes. He told of Naim Fraseri, the poet, and Skënderbej, the brave general. He told stories of the proud people who were called Shqipëtar—People of the Eagle.

The little group always made a special stop. Everyone, even Shega, was quiet as Gjyshi put his finger to his lips and said "Shhh!" Quickly, they stepped off the path and tied Shega to a tree branch. Nëna took her basket filled with food, and in a flash they slipped inside an old house that was set back from the road.

17

Two old people lived in the little house. Both of them were stooped and tired from many years of working in the fields. First Gjyshi and Nëna approached the old man with outstretched hands. They kissed his right hand slowly and reverently, and the old man said some quiet words and touched their heads. Nëna handed the basket to the old woman and hugged her tightly. Then they said goodbye and went on their way.

Every week of every summer they visited the old man and woman. Gjyshi and Nëna always cautioned them to tell no one. Every time it was the same.

But last year it was different. After Nëna handed the old woman the basket, the woman reached her hand toward Drita. Drita looked into her gentle brown eyes and felt such a peaceful and happy feeling. The old woman held onto Drita's hand and in her soft voice said, "Drita, your name means 'light.' God is Light. He sent His only Son so that we may live in the Light. God is with us." And then the small group turned and silently went back to Shega.

The rest of the afternoon, Gjyshi was very quiet. When they arrived home, he tied Shega to the fence, patted his shaggy head, and called the children to him. Tears ran down his cheeks.

"Children," Gjyshi started, "did you hear what the old woman said to us today? We live in a country whose government has destroyed our churches and forbidden us to teach our children about Jesus Christ. They have burnt our icons and our Bibles. They have humiliated our priests and made them suffer like old Papa Kristo. Christians have gone to prison and died for their faith. But times are changing. A new government is certain to be coming. We will once again be able to remember the faith of our fathers and grandfathers."

"But Gjyshi," Drita said, "we are not Christians. It is against the law to be Christian. All of the Christians are in prison."

Gjyshi went inside, took a family picture that hung on the wall, and turned it over in his big hands. A few times Drita had awakened at night to see her grandparents standing in front of that picture. She remembered that when she stirred, Gjyshi would reach up and quickly turn the picture over.

Now, Gjyshi and Nëna had tears in their eyes as they gently held the picture in their rough hands. They turned the picture over, took the cardboard covering off the back, and kissed it tenderly. Drita and Artan saw the large, kind eyes of a young man looking back at them. His head was covered in a crown of thorns and his hands were tied. Even though he looked as if he were hurt, his eyes were gentle and loving. "Children, it is time for you to know the truth. We are

Christians. Those who have persecuted us are losing power. There are uprisings and stirrings of the people. Soon we will be free to worship and pray to our Lord and Savior Jisu Krisht.

"Old Papa Kristo and Prifteresa Marika, whom we visit every week, have prayed that you may one day know about our Holy Orthodox faith."

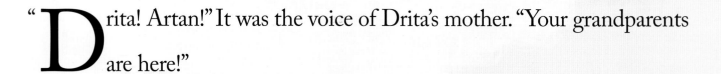

"Drita! Artan!" It was the voice of Drita's mother. "Your grandparents are here!"

Drita looked up from her daydreaming. Her grandparents were standing on the front steps of the church. Next to them were their friends Papa Kristo and Prifteresa Marika. What a special joy! Drita and Artan ran to hug everyone.

"Papa Kristo will help the Archbishop with the sacrament," added Gjyshi.

When Drita greeted Papa Kristo, she reverently kissed his right hand as she remembered her grandparents doing every summer. Drita's joy seemed to fill her whole heart. She was thankful for the people who had secretly kept their faith during the years when it had been illegal to be Christian in Albania. She was thankful for Archbishop Anastasios, who was leading the Orthodox Church in Albania into a new time of religious freedom.

Drita entered the church in her white baptismal garment and thought she was the luckiest girl in the entire world. She would be able to take Holy Communion and be part of the Church that her grandparents and great-grandparents had belonged to.

The Archbishop came out of the altar in flowing white robes with Papa Kristo, and the service began.

Before Drita was immersed in the warm water of the baptismal font, she looked at her smiling grandmother. She thought of the sweet-tasting well water in the village and of the icon her grandmother had kept hidden all those years. Then she remembered the stories that Nëna had told her about Saint Paul, the missionary who had traveled the world. Maybe someday Drita would be a missionary too, just like Saint Paul.

Some Albanian words to know

Ati ynë: "Our Father," the name of the Lord's prayer

Babi: Dad or Daddy

Besorja: "I believe," the name of the Creed

gjizë: A cottage cheese made from yogurt

Gjyshi: Grandfather, also a respectful way to address an older man

haide: "Come on" or "let's go." Many countries in the region use the same word.

Hoxha: Communist dictator who ruled Albania after World War II

       until his death in 1985

Jisu Krisht: Jesus Christ

Mami: Mom or Mommy

Nëna: Grandmother, also a respectful way to address an older woman

Papa: Familiar term to address an Orthodox priest

Prifteresa: Familiar term to address the wife of the priest

✟ *Historical Note* ✟

Writing to the Romans in about AD 55, St. Paul shares that "from Jerusalem and round about to Illyricum I have fully preached the gospel of Christ" (Romans 15:19). Today Illyricum is known as Albania. The Orthodox Church flourished there for centuries until it faced two waves of extreme religious persecution. The first wave lasted for almost five hundred years under the Ottoman Empire. Then in this century a second wave came under a very strict communist government.

Under communism, Albania closed its borders and declared all forms of religion constitutionally illegal. Many clergy were persecuted, some were imprisoned, some were publicly shaven and their vestments burned in front of them while tractors knocked down their churches. In order to discover who was keeping the faith, during the weeks surrounding the celebration of Pascha, school teachers would ask their students if they had any knowledge of a rare disease that affected the color of chicken eggs. If any students had seen anyone eat eggs with red shells, they were to immediately tell the teacher so that "medical help" could be sent. In 1991–92, the communist regime finally collapsed, and Archbishop Anastasios was sent to Albania by the Ecumenical Patriarch to resurrect the Orthodox Church.

It is during this transition that the story of Drita begins. We see Drita's grandparents finally being able to share their faith with their grandchildren. They no longer fear the repercussions of seven years of harsh prison terms if they were to be turned in to the authorities for being Christian. Since the fall of communism, hundreds of clergy have been trained, tens of thousands of baptisms have been performed, and hundreds of the 1,608 destroyed churches and monasteries have been rebuilt. The name Drita means 'light' in Albanian, and it is symbolic of the Light of Christ, which now shines in that land. ✟